Mitt Magic

Mitt Magic

FINGERPLAYS FOR FINGER PUPPETS

By Lynda Roberts
Illustrations by James Morris

gryphon
house inc.

ISBN Number 0—87659—111—X

Publishers Note: Teachers wanting ready made finger puppet sets may be interested in the "Monkey Mitt" * and many different finger puppet sets manufactured by the Wizard of Ahhs and available from most early childhood suppliers and school supply systems.

*"Monkey Mitt" is a registered trademark of The Wizard of Ahhs, Inc.

ACKNOWLEDGEMENTS

The fingerplays in this book are a varied collection. Some are from the folk tradition; I can take personal credit for authoring some; and some were created by other individuals; but most I have simply absorbed over my years of teaching. I only hope that what you find in this book will bring pleasure to you and to the children you teach. I want to thank Alberta Miller, Jeri Jensen, Marian Dunnick, Louise Knostman and all my friends and associates who have contributed to this collection.

INTRODUCTION

This book is a collection of fingerplays based on the number five. Both teachers and parents will find many ways to use these verses with young children. They can be read aloud by an adult, or acted out with the fingers by adult and child. (The Directions are found on page 73.) The glove and puppets add a visual component to the child's experience with the words. I have found that preschool children have a delightful sense of humor. When you say a verse such as "Five Enormous Dinosaurs", (page 28), and it turns out that the enormous dinosaurs are finger—tip size, you will quickly see this sense of humor and delight. The tiny puppets also add texture and the sense of touch to the child's experience. My five little squirrels (page 15) have tails of real fur, and my five little seashells (page 60) are real shells attached to the glove with Velcro. I also use real bells (page 69) with Velcro sewed to the red ribbon.

Fingerplays are a perfect way to encourage active participation by the children in your classroom. The simplest possibility is to have the children act out the story on their fingers; another possibility is to ask a child to remove the figures from the glove as the fingerplay is read. "Five Little Valentines" (page 54), and "Five Little Donuts" (page 29) are fun to use this way. When I have five children in front of the class holding the fingertip figures, I repeat the fingerplay, asking these children to pick the next participants. When we are done, the ones holding the figures come up and put them back on the glove. This is an excellent small muscle, hand—eye coordination exercise, especially for very young children.

Children will enjoy using the gloves and puppets themselves, and a glove with a set of figures makes a wonderful present. After hearing the fingerplays a few times, most children will be delighted to show you the story by themselves.

Towards the end of the book, I share other ideas for involving young children in the story telling process. All of these ideas can be used with the fingerplays in this collection, and they also can be adapted very successfully for use with other simple stories. The different kinds of masks (illustrated on page 75) are fun for everyone. They can be made either by the children or by an adult. I have delightful pictures of the children I teach being the five speckled frogs (page 33), and the five little pumpkins (page 64). If your children need to do a skit or song for a parent meeting, this can be a simple presentation which needs little preparation. Parents will be delighted, and tne children will enjoy the opportunity to please them.

The tongue depressor stick puppets (page 75, figure B) are simple to make and to use. The illustrations in the book can be enlarged, if necessary, or, in the case of the clowns (page 43), the firefighters (page 45), and the police officers (page 46), I have made a Xerox copy, then colored the figures, covered them with clear contact paper, and attached them to the tongue depressors. These make very durable visual aids which can be used in a variety of ways. Sometimes I hold them myself, but when I recite "Five Little Bees", (page 23), I often choose five children to hold the bees. I tell them to get into their beehive (make a circle), then I suggest where

they should buzz to; for example, buzz to the door, then back to their places. This is generally followed by, "Let's do it again, teacher!". I do try to be sure that every child who wants one has a turn. Remember that not all of the children will want a turn, and that you don't have to give everyone his or her turn on the same day. The same fingerplays can be done for a week, or more. Children love repetition, and, after a few days, a child who would not have participated earlier may be ready for a turn. The teacher will often become bored with the activity long before the children will.

The fingerplays can be used as flannel board stories. Since only five characters are necessary, they are a good introduction to the flannel board for young children. The illustrations should be enlarged, then transferred onto pellon or felt. The teacher can place these on the flannel board, or take them off, depending on the story; or the children can do this. When you are using the flannel board for counting activities, it is important to remember that the pieces should be placed on the board from left to right. You are always modelling the reading process for the children.

Counting and early math learning go hand in hand. A five year old child should have number concept to five, and a much younger child may be able to master number concept to five. The manipulation of real objects is one important way that a child masters the concept of number. More complex math concepts can also be taught with these simple fingerplays. When there are five little ducks, and one goes away (page 30), the idea of subtraction is being introduced. When

one little bird finds a friend (page 24), I have introduced addition. And if I take the donuts (page 29) and the pennies (page 39) and combine them, I illustrate one to one correspondence. Math, experienced this way, as a natural part of the world, is easy and fun.

Language skills, too, will benefit from the use of these verses. The children I teach come to school with various experiences and from diverse backgrounds. Some of them know very little spoken English. I have found that when I use fingerplays, illustrated in a variety of ways, the children gain significantly, both in vocabulary and in their ability to conceptualize. New words are introduced and spoken English is increased by the students' participation.

Fingerplays are a useful tool for the teacher in a practical way, as well, for they help to get the children's attention. In my classroom, I have found that children like surprises. When I tell them there is something different on my glove today, I know that they will be curious and interested. If I tell them we are going to do a familiar fingerplay in a new way, I have their attention. Only when I have their attention can I teach them.

In closing, let me remind you of a familiar saying, which can help us all to be better teachers. "I hear, and I forget; I see, and I remember; I do, and I understand."

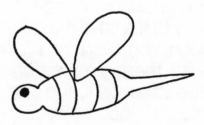

CONTENTS

SECTION I. FINGERPLAYS FOR EVERY DAY

SECTION II. FINGERPLAYS FOR SPECIAL HOLIDAYS

FINGERPLAYS FOR EVERY DAY

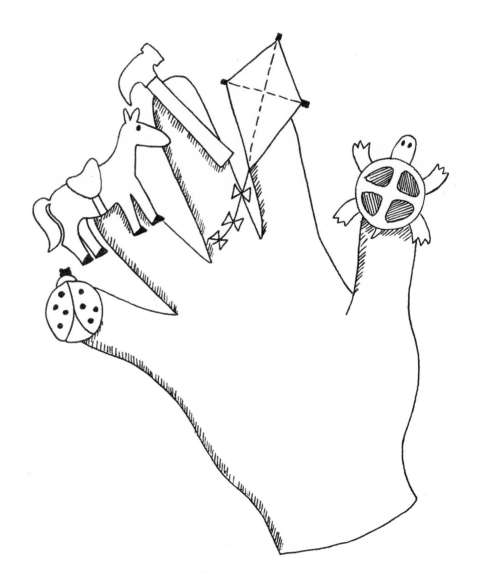

SQUIRRELS

Five little squirrels sitting in a tree.
The first one said, "What do I see?"
The second one said, "Some nuts on the
   ground."
The third one said, "Those are nuts I found."
The fourth one said, "I'll race you there."
The fifth one said, "All right, that's fair."
So they shook their tails and ran with glee!
To the nuts that lay at the foot of the tree.

ENGINE ON THE TRACK

Here is the engine on the track. *(Hold up thumb)*
Here is the coal car, just in back. *(Pointer)*
Here is the box car to carry freight. *(Middle)*
Here is the mail car. Don't be late. *(Ring)*
Way back here at the end of the train. *(Little)*
Rides the caboose through the sun and rain.

TURTLES

One baby turtle alone and new,
Finds a friend, and then there are two.
Two baby turtles crawl down to the sea.
They find another, and then there are three.
Three baby turtles crawl along the shore.
They find another, and then there are four.
Four baby turtles go for a dive.
Up swims another, and then there are five.

GET A TICKET

Get a ticket, ticket, ticket for the train.
Get a ticket, ticket, ticket for the train.
Don't stand out in the wind and rain.
Get a ticket, ticket, ticket for the train.

Verse 2. Bus: Climb aboard, you can ride with us.
Verse 3. Plane: Don't stand out in the wind and
rain.
Verse 4. Boat: The water's too cold to swim or
float.
Verse 5. Bike: It's way too far to walk or hike.

PURPLE VIOLETS

One purple violet in our garden grew.
Up popped another, and that made two.

Two purple violets were all that I could see;
But _____ found another, and that
    made three.

Three purple violets—if _____ could
    find one more,
We'd give them to mother—we'd have four!

Four purple violets—sure as you're alive!
Why, here is another! And now there are five!

(Children place violets on flannel board, in turn.)

THE ZOO

At the zoo we saw a bear.
He had long, dark, fuzzy hair.

We saw a lion in a cage.
He was in an awful rage.

We saw the big, long-necked giraffe,
And the silly monkeys made us laugh.

But my favorite animal at the zoo
Is the elephant—how about you?

FIVE TEDDY BEARS

One little teddy bear, finding things to do.
Along came another. Then there were two.

Two busy teddy bears, climbing up to see.
Along came another. Then there were three.

Three lively teddy bears liked to explore.
Along came another. Then there were four.

Four hungry teddy bears, eating honey from a
   hive.
Along came another. Then there were five.

Five tired honey bears had fun today.
They'll be back tomorrow, and you can see them
   play.

FIVE LITTLE BEES

One little bee flew and flew.
He met a friend, and that made two.

Two little bees, busy as could be—
Along came another and that made three.

Three little bees wanted one more,
Found one soon and that made four.

Four little bees, going to the hive,
Spied their little brother, and that made five.

Five little bees working every hour—
Buzz away, bees, and find another flower.

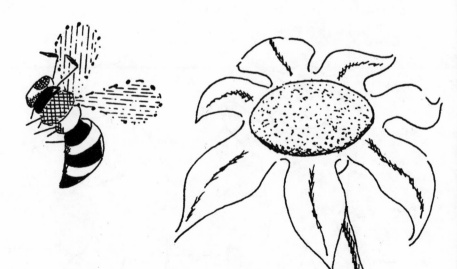

BEES

Here is the beehive,
But where are all the bees?

Hidden away
Where nobody sees.

Soon they'll come
Creeping out of the hive.

ONE
  TWO
    THREE
      FOUR
        FIVE

(Have your hand closed at the beginning of the rhyme - open the fingers one by one as you count to five.)

BIRDS

There was one little bird in a little tree,
He was all alone, and he didn't want to be.
So he flew far away, over the sea,
And brought back a friend to live in the tree.

*(Substitute two, three, four and five for one as
you finish the verse, adding one more bird each
time to the mitt.)*

JINNY BIRDS

Five little Jinny birds, hopping by my door—
One went to build a nest, and then there were
  four.

Four little Jinny birds singing lustily—
One got out of tune, and then there were three.

Three little Jinny birds, and what should one do,
But go in search of dinner, leaving only two.

Two little Jinny birds singing for fun—
One flew far away, and then there was one.

One little Jinny bird sitting in the sun—
He took a little nap, and then there was none.

CHICKADEES

Five little chickadees, sitting by a door—
One flew away, and then there were four.

CHORUS:
Chickadees, chickadees, happy and gay,
Chickadees, chickadees, fly away.

Four little chickadees, sitting in a tree—
One flew away, and then there were three.

Chorus

Three little chickadees, looking at you—
One flew away, and then there were two.

Chorus

Two little chickadees, sitting in the sun—
One flew away, and then there was one.

Chorus

One little chickadee, sitting all alone—
That one flew away, and then there was none.

FIVE LITTLE ROBINS

Five little robins lived in a tree—
Father, mother, and babies three.
Father caught a worm.
Mother caught a bug.
The three little robins began to tug.
This one got a bug.
This one got a worm.
This one said, "Now it's my turn."

*(Start with a fist. Raise fingers, beginning with
the thumb: "Father caught a worm" . . . etc.
Point to index finger, etc. when "This one got a
bug.")*

DINOSAURS

Five enormous dinosaurs
Letting out a roar—
One went away, and
Then there were four.

Four enormous dinosaurs
Crashing down a tree—
One went away, and
Then there were three.

Three enormous dinosaurs
Eating tiger stew—
One went away, and
Then there were two.

Two enormous dinosaurs
Trying to run—
One ran away, and
Then there was one.

One enormous dinosaur,
Afraid to be a hero—
He went away, and
Then there was zero.

FIVE DONUTS

Five little donuts in a bakery shop,
Sprinkled with powdered sugar on top.
Along comes *(insert name of child)* with a penny
   to pay.
He buys a donut and takes it away.
(Continue with four, three, two and one.)

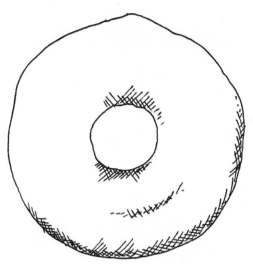

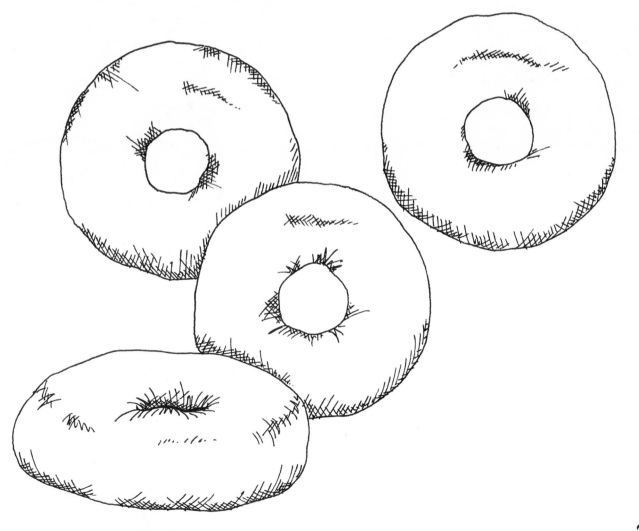

FIVE YELLOW DUCKLINGS

Five yellow ducklings
Went swimming one day,
Across the pond
And far away.

Old mother duck said,
"Quack, quack, quack."
Four yellow ducklings
Came swimming back.

(Continue until there is one left.)

One yellow duckling
Went swimming one day,
Across the pond
And far away.

Old mother duck said,
"Quack, quack, quack."
No yellow ducklings
Came swimming back.

Old mother duck said,
"Quack, quack, quack."
(Say very loud)
Five yellow ducklings
Came swimming back.

FIVE LITTLE FISHES

Five little fishes swimming in a pool—
This one said, "The pool is cool."
This one said, "The pool is deep."
This one said, "I'd like to sleep."
This one said, "I'll float and dip."
This one said, "I see a ship."
The fishing boat comes.
The line goes splash.
All the little fishes swim away in a flash!

FISH

(Insert child's name in the blank.)

There are so many fish in the deep blue sea
What color fish does _____ see?

(Put a different colored fish on each finger one at a time.)

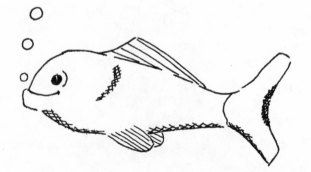

FIVE LITTLE SPECKLED FROGS

Five little speckled frogs,
Sitting on a speckled log,
Eating the most delicious bugs—yum, yum.
One jumped into the pool
Where it was nice and cool.
Then there were four speckled frogs.

(Continue until one is left)

One little speckled frog,
Sitting on a speckled log,
Eating the most delicious bugs—yum, yum.
He jumped into the pool
Where it was nice and cool.
Now there are no speckled frogs.

FIVE LITTLE FROGGIES

Five little froggies sitting on a well—
One looked up, and down he fell.
   Froggies jumped high.
   Froggies jumped low.

Four little froggies sitting on a well—
One looked up, and down he fell.
   Froggies jumped high.
   Froggies jumped low.

Three little froggies sitting on a well—
One looked up, and down he fell.
   Froggies jumped high.
   Froggies jumped low.

Two little froggies sitting on a well—
One looked up, and down he fell.
   Froggies jumped high.
   Froggies jumped low.

One little froggy sitting on a well—
He looked up, and down he fell.

JOHNNY POUNDS WITH ONE HAMMER

Johnny pounds with one hammer, one hammer, one hammer.
Johnny pounds with one hammer, now he pounds with two.
Johnny pounds with two hammers, two hammers, two hammers.

(Repeat until you have no hammers.)

Now he STOPS!

(Whole body activity. On one hammer, children pound with one fist, then two. Then two fists and one foot. Then two fists and two feet. Then two fists and two feet and nod the head. Other parts of the body can be substituted at the suggestion of the teacher or the children.)

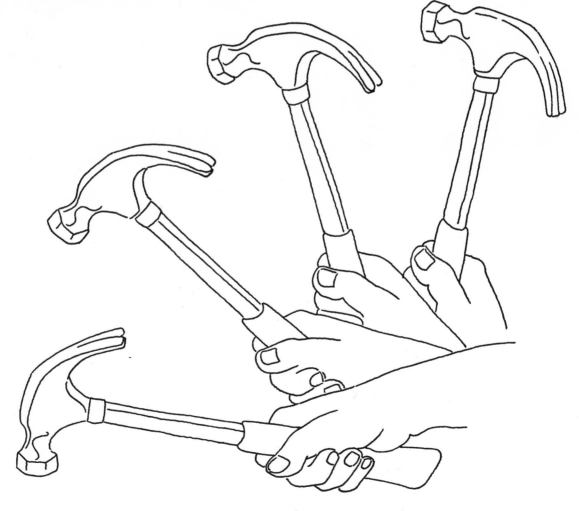

LADY BUGS

I saw a little lady bug flying in the air,
But when I tried to catch her, two bugs were
 there.

Two little lady bugs flew up in a tree.
I tiptoed very quietly, and then I saw three.
Three little lady bugs—I looked for one more.
I saw one sitting on the ground: that made four.

Four little lady bugs—another one arrived.
I saw her sitting on a flower, and that made five.

Five little lady bugs, all red and black—
I clapped my hands and shouted, and they all
flew back!

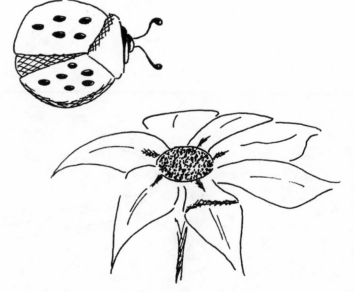

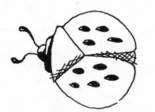

MONKEYS IN A TREE

Five little monkeys
Sitting in a tree
Teasing Mr. Crocodile—
"You can't catch me."
"You can't catch me."

Along comes Mr. Crocodile
As quiet as can be—
SNAP!!!!

(Continue until all monkeys are gone)
Finish with—

Away swims Mr. Crocodile
As full as he can be!!!!

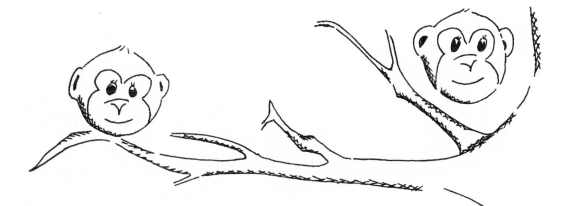

MONKEYS ON A BED

Five little monkeys
Jumping on a bed.

One fell off and bumped his head.

Mama called the doctor,
And the doctor said,

"Keep those monkeys off that bed!"

Four little monkeys . . . ..
(Repeat until none are left.)

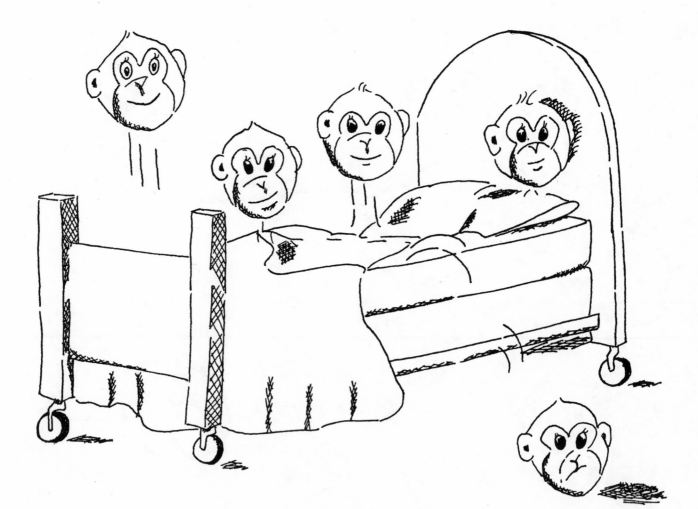

MICE

Five little mice on the pantry floor—
This little mouse peeked behind the door
This little mouse nibbled at the cake.
This little mouse made the pitcher break.
This little mouse found some cheese.
This little mouse heard the kitten sneeze.
"Ah choo!" sneezed the kitten. "Squeak!" the
    mouse cried.
They found a hole, and they ran inside.

FIVE LITTLE PENNIES

Five little pennies—I took them to the store.
I bought a peppermint; then there were four.

Four little pennies belong just to me.
One bought a pencil; then there were three.

Three little pennies—I'll share them with you.
One bought a lemon drop; then there were two.

Two little pennies as bright as the sun—
One bought a marble; then there was one.

One little penny was all I had to pay.
I put it in my piggy bank for a rainy day!

FIVE LITTLE BABIES

One little baby rocking in a tree.
Two little babies splashing in the sea.
Three little babies crawling on the floor.
Four little babies banging on the door.
Five little babies playing hide n' seek.
Close your eyes now 'til I say, "Peek!"

FIVE LITTLE BABIES

Five little babies
Say, "Goodnight"
Five little babies
Stand upright.

You must lie down
If you want to sleep.
You must lie still
Without a peep.

First is the little one—
Down he goes.
Down he goes
On his little red nose.

The second one says,
"I'm tired too;
You don't mind
If I lie near you?"

Then comes the third,
The tallest one.
"I like to sleep.
It's a lot of fun."

Down he goes
And that makes three
Sleeping
Very quietly.

Now let's look
At the other two.
One's tall, one's small,
And then there's you.

First the tall one
Bends his head.
Then the small one
Goes to bed.

That leaves you
And you're the best.
Goodnight, dear!
It's time to rest.

(Great for rest time or bedtime.)

THIS LITTLE CLOWN

The first little clown is
fat and gay.
The second little clown does
tricks all day.
The third little clown is
tall and strong.
The fourth little clown
sings a funny song.
The fifth little clown is
wee and small,
But he can do anything,
anything at all!

FIVE LITTLE GIRLS

Five little girls woke up in their beds.
    (curl fingers loosely in palm)

This little girl jumped right out of bed.
    *(starting with thumb, let each finger pop up
    for one girl)*
This little girl shook her curly head.
This little girl washed her sleepy face.
This little girl put all her clothes in place.
This little girl put on her shoes and socks.
And they all ran down to breakfast
When the time was eight o'clock.
    (all fingers run behind back)

FIVE LITTLE FIREFIGHTERS

Five little firefighters sit very still.
(Hold up five fingers.)
Until they see a fire on top of the hill.
Number one rings the bell, ding-dong.
(Bend down thumb.)
Number two pulls his big boots on.
(Bend down pointer finger.)
Number three climbs on the truck right away.
(Bend down middle finger.)
Number four joins him—no one can wait.
(Bend down ring finger)
Number five drives the truck to the fire.
(Bend down little finger.)
The big yellow flames go higher and higher.
(Spread arms.)
Whooo—ooo! Whooo—ooo! Hear the fire truck
   say
(Imitate siren.)
As all of the cars get out of the way.
Shhh! goes the water from the fire hose spout,
(Rub palms together)
And quicker than a wink the fire is out!
(Clap hands.)

POLICE OFFICERS

Five police officers standing by a door—
One became a traffic cop; then there were four.
Four police officers watching over me—
One took home a lost boy, and then there were
 three.
Three police officers dressed all in blue—
One stopped a speeding car, and then there
 were two.
Two police officers—how fast they run!
One caught a bad man, and then there was one.
One police officer saw smoke faraway.
He called the firehouse, and the firemen saved
 the day.

PIGGIES

"It's time for my piggies to go to bed,"
The great big mother piggy said.
"So I will count them first to see
If all my piggies came back to me.
One little piggy, two little piggies, three little
    piggies dear.
Four little piggies, five little piggies—yes, they're
    all here!"

CIRCUS PONIES

Five circus ponies all in a row—
One jumped through a hoop, and now there are
  four.

Four circus ponies standing by a tree—
One walked away, and now there are three.

Three circus ponies waiting for their cue—
One danced about, and now there are two.

Two circus ponies thought they were done.
One dashed away, and now there is one.

One circus pony standing all alone—
He took a bow, and went on home.

FINGERPLAYS FOR SPECIAL HOLIDAYS

BALLOONS FOR A PARTY

Here are balloons for a party,
For it is my birthday today.
I have balloons for all my friends
Who are coming over to play.

Here is a pretty, round, blue balloon,
Blue as my kitten's eyes.

Here is a flaming, round, red balloon,
Just about your size.

Here is a happy, round, yellow balloon,
Yellow as bright sunshine.

Here is a lovely, round, purple balloon
Like purple grapes on a vine.

Here is a little, round, orange balloon
Like oranges from a store.

And now there are no more.

*(As each balloon is mentioned, hand
it to a child in the circle.)*

FIVE CANDLES

Five candles on a birthday cake—
five, and not one more—
You may blow one candle out, *(-wh-)*
and that leaves four!
Four candles on a birthday cake
for all to see—
You may blow one candle out, *(-wh-)*
and that leaves three!
Three candles on a birthday cake,
standing straight and true—
You may blow one candle out, *(-wh-)*
and that leaves two!
Two candles on a birthday cake
helping us have fun—
You may blow one candle out, *(-wh-)*
and that leaves one!
One candle on a birthday cake—
we know its task is done.
You may blow this candle out, *(-wh-)*
and that leaves none!

SNOWMEN

Five little snowmen standing round my door—
This one melted, and then there were four.

Four little snowmen beneath a green tree—
This one melted, and then there were three.

Three little snowmen all have mittens blue.
This one melted, and then there were two.

Two little snowmen standing in the sun—
This one melted, and then there was one.

One little snowman wanted to run,
But he melted away, and then there was none.

FIVE VALENTINES

Five cheerful valentines from the ten cent
store—
    I sent one to _____; now I have four.

Four cheerful valentines, pretty ones to see—
    I gave one to _____; now I have three.

Three cheerful valentines with flowers pink and
blue—
    I gave one to _____; now I have two.

Two cheerful valentines—my story's almost
done.
    I gave one to _____; now I have one.

One cheerful valentine—one and only one—
    I gave it to _____; now I have none.

(Insert a child's name in each blank space.)

KITES

Five little kites flying high in the sky
Said, "Hi!" to the cloud as it passed by,
Said, "Hi!" to the bird, said "Hi!" to the sun,
Said, "Hi!" to an airplane—oh what fun!
Then whish went the wind,
And they all took a dive:

ONE
  TWO
    THREE
      FOUR
        FIVE.

SHAMROCKS

Five little shamrocks lying in the grass—
Along came a leprechaun skipping down the
   path.
He took a shamrock and put it on a door.
That's for good luck, and that leaves four.

Four little shamrocks lying in the grass—
Along came a leprechaun skipping down the
   path.
He pinned on a shamrock for all to see.
That's for good luck, and now there are three.

Three little shamrocks lying in the grass—
Along came a leprechaun skipping down the
   path.
He picked one up and put it in his shoe.
That's for good luck, and now there are two.

Two little shamrocks lying in the grass—
Along came a leprechaun skipping down the
   path.
He picked one up and held it toward the sun.
That's for good luck, and now there's only one.

One little shamrock lying in the grass—
Along came a leprechaun skipping down the
   path.
He left it lying there so there'd always be one.
That's for good luck—can you find one?

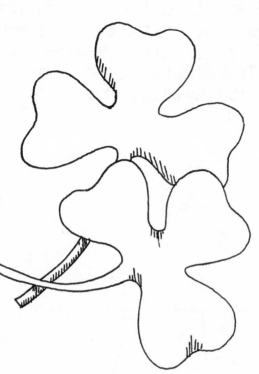

EASTER RABBITS

Five Easter rabbits standing by the door—
One hopped away, and then there were four.

Four Easter rabbits sitting near a tree—
One hopped away, and then there were three.

Three Easter rabbits looking at you—
One hopped away, and then there were two.

Two Easter rabbits enjoying the sun—
One hopped away, and then there was one.

One Easter rabbit sitting all alone—
He hopped away, and then there were none!

EASTER EGGS

On Easter morning the sun comes up,
Round and yellow as a buttercup.

The sun is shining, the air is still,
And the Easter rabbit hops over the hill.

Here's my basket. Let's go see
If the rabbit left Easter eggs for me.

Here is a yellow one, yellow as the sun!
I'll put it in my basket. That makes one.

Here is a green one, right by my shoe!
I'll put it in my basket. That makes two!

Here is a purple one, hidden carefully!
I'll put it in my basket. That makes three!

Here is a red one—Easter eggs galore!
I'll put it in my basket. That makes four.

Here is a blue one, blue as the sky.
I'll put it in my basket. That makes five.

My basket is full now. Let's go home.
I'd like to sit down and give you some.

FIVE MAY BASKETS

Five May baskets waiting by the door—
One will go to _____. Then there will be
four.

Four May baskets, pretty as can be—
One will go to _____. Then there will be
three.

Three May baskets—one is pink and blue.
One will go to _____. Then there will be
two.

Two May baskets waiting in the sun—
One will go to _____. Then there will be
one.

One May basket—I want it to go
To my own dear mother. She's the nicest one I
know.

*(Insert a child's name in each
blank space.)*

FIVE LITTLE SEASHELLS

(Hold up five fingers, and swish each one down with other hand.)

Five little seashells lying on the shore—
Swish went the waves, and then there were four.
Four little seashells, pretty as could be—
Swish went the waves, and then there were
   three.
Three little seashells all pearly new—
Swish went the waves, and then there were two.
Two little seashells shining in the sun—
Swish went the waves, and then there was one.
One little seashell left all alone—
I picked it up, and I took it home.

AUTUMN LEAVES

Five little leaves in the autumn breeze
Tumbled and fluttered from the trees.
The first little leaf said, "I am red,
I shall rest on a flower bed."
The second little leaf, an orange one, said,
"Pick me up! I'm cold and wet."
The third little leaf said, "I am yellow.
I'm a happy-go-lucky fellow."
The fourth little leaf said, "I'm still as green
As when I was part of the summer scene."
The fifth little leaf said, "I am brown,
And I shall blow all over town."

FIVE LITTLE GHOSTS

Five little ghosts
Went out to play.
A great big pumpkin looked at them,
And one little ghost ran away.

Four little ghosts
Went out to play.
A scary skeleton tip—toed by,
And one little ghost ran away.

Three little ghosts
Went out to play.
An ugly witch came riding by,
And one little ghost ran away.

Two little ghosts
Went out to play.
A big black cat looked at them,
And one little ghost ran away.

One little ghost
Went out to play.
A gobbling goblin shrieked by,
And that little ghost ran away.

FIVE LITTLE GOBLINS

Five little goblins on a Halloween night
Made a very spooky sight.
The first two danced on their tippy, tippy toes.
The next one jumped high. Up he goes!
The last two sang a Halloween song.
The five little goblins played the whole night
    long.

FIVE LITTLE PUMPKINS

Five little pumpkins were sitting on a gate.
The first one said, "It's getting mighty late."
The second one said, "There are witches in the
    air."
The third one said, "I really don't care."
The fourth one said, "Let's run, run, run."
The fifth one said, "It's Halloween fun."
"Whooo" went the wind, and out went the light,
And the five little pumpkins rolled out of sight.

LITTLE WITCHES

Five little witches on Halloween night—
The first one whispered, "Time for our flight."
The second one whispered, "The moon's bright
  as day."
The third one whispered, "It's so far away!"
The fourth one whispered, "It's just across the
  sky."
The fifth one whispered, "Up brooms and fly!"

THANKSGIVING CHILDREN

This may be done as a spoken verse and fingerplay. It can also be adapted to the tune, "Up On the Housetop," and used with the finger puppets.

Five little children on Thanksgiving Day—
The first one said, "I'd like cake if I may."
The second one said, "I'd like turkey roasted."
The third one said, "I'd like chestnuts toasted."
The fourth one said, "I'd like pumpkin pie."
The fifth one said, "Oh, so would I!"
But before they ate the turkey or the dressing,
Five little children said the Thanksgiving blessing.

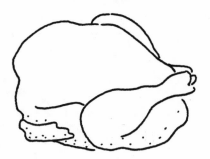

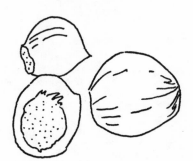

FIVE TURKEYS

Five big turkeys sitting on the gate—
The first one said, "It's getting late."

Chorus:
Gobble, gobble, gobble
Fat turkeys, fat turkeys
Gobble, gobble, gobble
Fat turkeys are we.

The second one said, "Who goes there?"
  Chorus
The third one said, "There are farmers
everywhere."
  Chorus
The fourth one said, "Let's run, run, run."
  Chorus
The fifth one said, "It's just Thanksgiving fun."
  Chorus

Five fat turkeys are we.
We slept all night in a tree.
When the cook came around,
We couldn't be found,
And that's why we're here, you see.

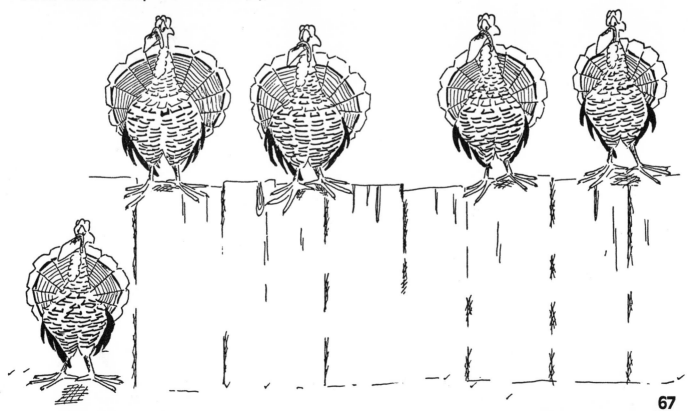

DREDEL

Dredel, dredel, dredel—see the spinning top.
I will set five spinning, and one will stop.

The green top is going 'round and 'round,
But it's the first top to hit the ground.

The red top is wobbling and wobbling now.
It is stopping to take a bow.

The yellow top is slowing a bit.
It stops when another top hits it.

The white and blue are turning still.
Which do you think can win at will?

The only one spinning is the top that's blue.
It's the one I give to you.

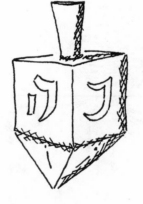
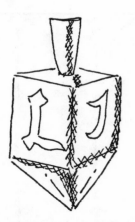

FIVE LITTLE BELLS

Five little bells ring with a chime.
They tell us of happy Christmas time.
Four little bells ring sweet and clear.
They tell us that Christmas Day is near.

Three little bells ring soft and low.
They tell us of stockings in a row.

Two little bells ring merrily.
They tell us of toys beneath the tree.

One little bell rings silver bright
To welcome Jesus on Christmas night.

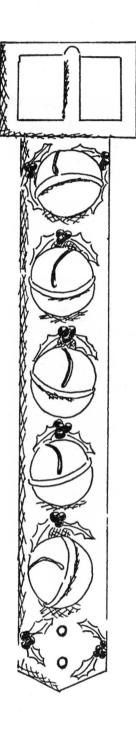

FIVE BRIGHT STARS

Five bright stars on Christmas night
Wanted to give their very best light.

The first one said, "I'll shine for the sheep
And the shepherds who their watch do keep.

The second one said, "I'll shine and see
If folks remember the prophecy."

The third one said, "I'll shine to show
The wise men just which way to go."

The fourth one said, "I'll shine to remind
People on earth to be good and kind."

The fifth one, brightest one of all,
Poured out its light 'til it reached a stall

Where shepherds and wise men knelt to pray
Beside the manger where Jesus lay.

The STAR OF THE EAST told all the earth
The wonderful news of the Savior's birth.

CHRISTMAS TREES

Five Christmas trees
In a forest green,
Waiting to be chosen,
Waiting to be seen.
Along came _____
To take one home—
A Christmas tree
For the family to see.

(As a flannel story, leave one side of tree undecorated, and child turns tree over to reveal decorations.)

FIVE RED STOCKINGS

Five red stockings heard the fire roar.
_____ took one. Then there were four.

Four red stockings by the Christmas tree—
_____ took one. Then there were three.

Three red stockings waiting for you—
_____ took one. Then there were two.

Two red stockings awaiting Christmas fun—
_____ took one. Then there was one.

The last red stocking was feeling kind of sad.
_____ took it, and we all were glad.

(Insert child's name where blank line is.)

DIRECTIONS FOR PUPPET GLOVE

1) Purchase a pair of white canvas garden gloves.

2) On one of the gloves (I am right-handed, but I use the glove on my left hand), sew a small square of Velcro on the finger tips of all the fingers, including the thumb (palm side). You are now ready to make your figures. (See Figure A.)

3) Trace the outline of set of patterns in the book.

4) Cut ten outline pieces out of felt or other firm material.

5) Sew Velcro fastener (opposite side as glove) to five of the pieces. (See Figure B.) This will be the back of the figure.

6) Decorate the other five pieces (the fronts) using appliques, permanent markers, felt, etc. (See Figure C.)

7) Join the two halves of each figure using your sewing machine or sewing by hand. Close only 3/4 of the way. (See Figure D.)

8) Stuff with a small amount of acrylic or a piece of a cotton ball. Finish sewing.

9) Pieces may also be made without stuffing by attaching Velcro directly to decorated piece.

10) I recommend that the Velcro be sewn on rather than glued. Sewing will make it more durable.

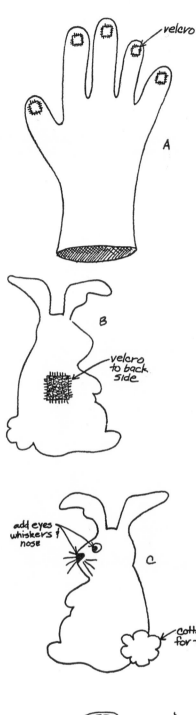

GLOSSARY OF IDEAS

Parents and teachers who have used the first edition of this book have suggested more ideas for using the figures in this book.

1) Paper bag masks to act out the fingerplays. (See Figure A.)

2) Tongue depressor stick puppets that can be used by the teacher or held by the children. These can be laminated or covered with clear contact paper for durability. (See Figure B.)

3) Paper plate puppets on a tongue depressor made by the teacher or the children. (See Figure C.)

4) Felt sleeve finger puppets. (See Figure D.)

5) Felt figures with a loop of elastic on the back. (See Figure E.)

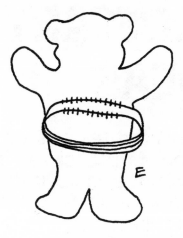

6) Whole body felt finger puppets. (See Figure F.)

7) Any cutout can become a finger puppet when a "T" is glued on the back. (See Figure H.)

8) Egg carton creature finger puppets. (See Figure G.)

Source: Scholastic Book - EGG CARTON CRITTERS

9) If you have a new idea for the use of fingerplays in FINGERPLAYS FOR FINGER PUPPETS, please send them to me in care of Gryphon House. All usable ideas will be included in the next edition.

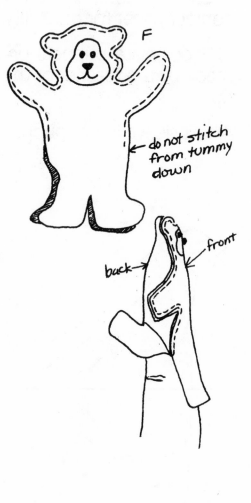

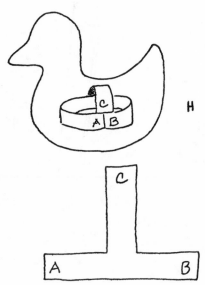

PATTERNS

15
Squirrels

16
Engine

18
Get a Ticket

17
Turtles

19
Purple Violets

20
The Zoo

21
Teddy Bears

22 23
Bees

24-27
Birds

28
Dinosaurs

30
Ducklings

31-32
Fish

37-38
Monkeys

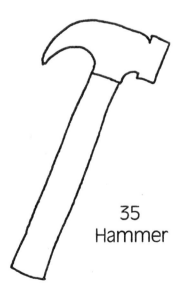

33-34
Frogs

35
Hammer

36
Lady Bugs

39
Mice

43
Clown

45
Firefighters

46
Police Officers

47
Piggies

48
Circus Ponies

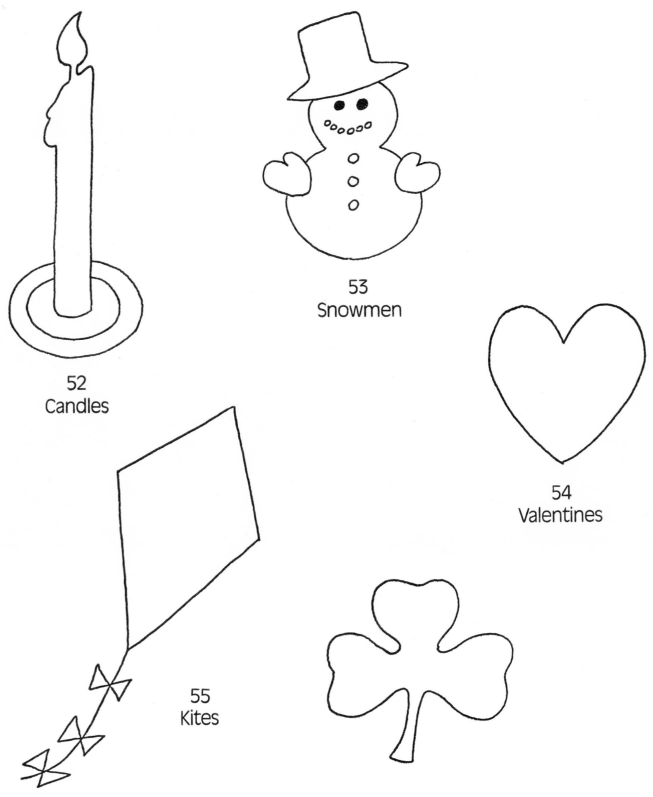

52
Candles

53
Snowmen

54
Valentines

55
Kites

56
Shamrocks

57
Rabbits

58
Eggs

59
May Baskets

61
Leaves

62–63
Ghosts-Goblins

64
Pumpkins

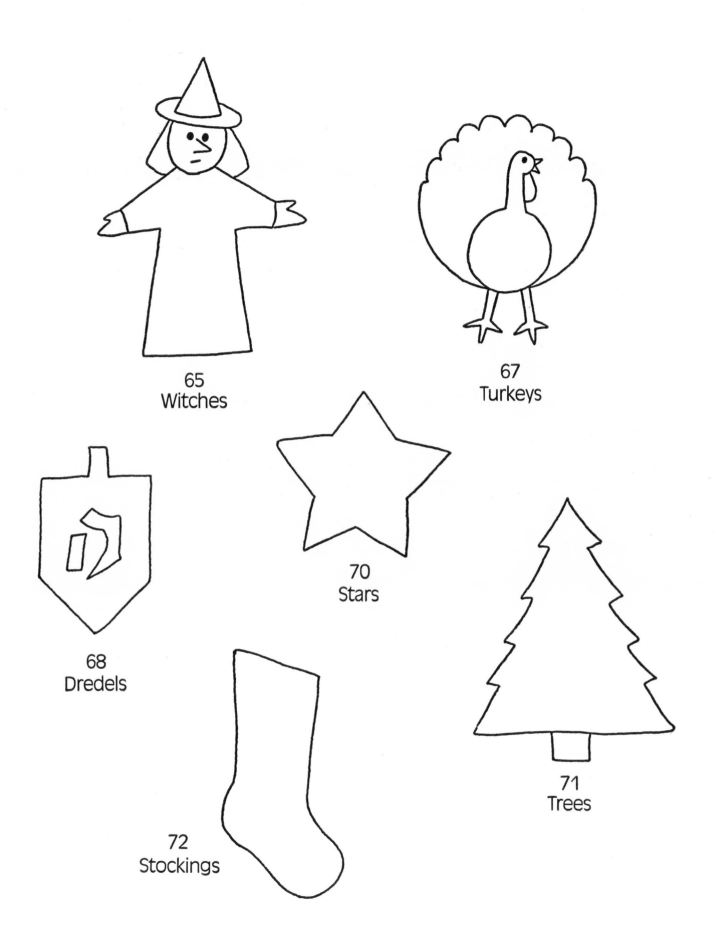

65
Witches

67
Turkeys

68
Dredels

70
Stars

71
Trees

72
Stockings